office life

Emma Lambert

Presentation by *BookLeaf Publishing*

Web: www.bookleafpub.com

E-mail: info@bookleafpub.com

ISBN: 9789357440905

First edition 2023

PREFACE

I'm tired of hearing how beautiful everywhere else is. I want to learn to see how amazing my everyday life already is and the adventure it can be.

morning commute

Morning commute what a daily dispute,

Trying not to smear my fresh makeup and my hair trying to frizz,

My stomach feels anxious but my fears I'm ready to spite!

Coffee hot in hand and in the passenger's seat my things dispersed,

The sun hasn't risen but we'll be working yet,

Traffic lights shine so bright, reflecting against the black road oh what a sight!

When on the road do us all the courtesy and push the limits for you see,

The lethargic and slow shouldn't mess with the morning traffics flow.

not enough sleep

Three hours makes my eyes cower,

In the light of my monitor my mind regrets,

The episodes watches last night many a day
could've covered,

Lack of energy I shake my head looking into my
coffee cup dregs,

I've got hours to go and many yawns I'll need to
cover up,

I feel dizzy in my chest and the crusty dry eyes,

A feeling too familiar to be easily given up,

Is this a problem? Probably not my mind
supplies.

reply to all

I'm in the groove typing fast and clearing my
queue,

Low and behold an email comes into view!

One blip on my radar ain't much isn't that true?

Back to it I aim to see this through,

Low and behold another email comes into view!

You've gone and replied to all, isn't that true?

All so everyone can see you've read this too,

I'm now out of the groove deleting fast and
judging this crew.

I run for me

The rhythmic thump of my shoes on the
treadmill,

Reminds me that I run for me, not you.

The gasping pants make my lungs tremble,

The battle of a body wanting to stumble,

Reminds me that this brings joy, it's true!

The itchiness under my skin crumbles,

The doubts in my mind are humbled,

Reminds me that I need to fight, just gotta get
through

And maybe my courage will be an inspiration
for you.

sunday

5

I walk through the doors of my church,

And find a healing balm for this week's wounds,

I come to God in prayer,

And hear His answer in His Word,

I fellowship with my brothers and sisters,

And find chances to lend a hand and be heard,

I awake on Monday morning,

And am ready to purpose hurry.

eight to four

Eight to four I've finally got control,

This is me living a dream come true,

I can finally send my stress on furlough,

The long stick is the one I drew,

The change of each minute my eyes no longer
follow,

All those long shifts I crawled through,

Now Sunday nights bring no more sorrow!

a traffic light

The fog of the morning blends with the traffic lights

It smooths the harsh lines, creates such magical sights

This one moment of man and nature blending in the heights

In my heart it fuels such delights

kids

Like the waves crashing upon the shore,

So is the play of little ones.

Unimaginable energy is bound in their core,

Frequent are their whines.

So many new emotions require lots of care,

Amongst these tiny humans peace wanes.

What a sacred call their little burdens to carry,

To set these future adults up for future wins,

And their current demons we toil to make cower.

above the dividers

Above the cubicle rises whispers,

Eager tones race to spread the tales,

With gleaming fangs and twisted whiskers,

Another's griefs they aim to tell!

Or maybe they're well wishers,

And they seek joy to till?

Or maybe they're truth twisters,

And they seek you to use as a tool,

So their path to attention is lessened of toil?

Or maybe all they offer is a trail of tolls,

All so your fine day they can foil?

holy spirit

You cannot run and you cannot hide,
The working of the Holy Spirit inevitable,

So stop putting off the call you will heed!
The mission we're set on is not too terrible,

So much I desire the victory that I've found a
holy greed!
For I run this race those words to be heard,
This taxing existence to be freed!

blue light filter

Phone screen you shine so bright,

In the darkness a beacon of light,

But sleep calls and it no longer should I fight,

Or tomorrow I'll be quite the sight,

And all those health videos would've been right!

i am a hopeful mess

I'm such a mess, I'll never progress;

I'm too pressed, doomed to regress!

My confidence is porous, my flaws I spot with prowess;

My doubts sing a chorus! But a peace of mind so precious,

Not just a premise but a promise,

Not a place but a process,

Not a pretense but a pursuance,

Is my Savior's presence in my present.

the office breakroom

Identifying an office breakroom isn't hard,

for starters two microwaves won't ever be far,

and a pile of napkins no doubt from somebody's
car,

will litter the counter with the required signing
of a strangers retirement card.

In the fridge that ancient ketchup still in a jar,

burnt into the carpet the smell of popcorn
charred,

and motivational sayings upon the wall never an
employee to charm.

tuesday

A random Tuesday afternoon,

Isn't that a beautiful thing?

Hours never too slow or too soon,

With wonder in even the simple ring.

In my heart an unexplainable urge to sing,

And in my mind a catchy tune,

I feel like I'll burst with anticipation at what
tomorrow is set to bring!

the micro manager

Like an ever watching eye,

Is the manager in the sky.

So anxiety is in vast supply,

As everyone is ready to try,

An escape through a lie.

Here comes another goodbye,

Another broken and ready to cry.

revenge insomnia

Oh that I had a switch in which I could shut my
mind off!

More than four hours for my body as I ought,

Instead of red eyes and lies of common sense
sought.

I'd be unstoppable and unswayable and in my
right mind I'd sit!

But instead of sleep so sweet and easy within my
sight,

When my head hits the bed the thoughts come
out to fight.

actually see

Look around and see there is magic to be found!

In coffee cup rings and other office things,

In flickers of light and plastic flowers,

In sticky notes and long nights,

In cup noodles and scrap paper doodles,

Even in old carpet and an atmosphere so corporate!

Nature and mankind are beautiful so near.

laundry

Like clockwork or the rising of the sun,

Up the stairs to the laundry I run,

Loads of cloths ready to go, oh what fun!

But how much more attractive the screen of a
phone,

Than the call of the responsible adult we all
feign.

In order to amongst our peers claim fame,

I'll lament my current state and hear them reply,
"same…"

For we all feel the fear of such a task so plain.

the migraine

Gaping wound within my mind,
Is there any relief to find?

An enemy before me that I can't run away from,
nor can any reinforcements to my aid come!

I must've been fleeing from the Lord,
For a tent peg has been driven through my head
to the floor.

It hurts but no words can do this pain justice,
The pain is real but I've no tears for this.

In this moment I fear I'd trade a limb for relief,
An arm to wither and fall as a tree's leaf.

The agony is here but it soon must end,
And on the other side I'll be amazed I didn't
bend.

For when the sun rises on this night,
I'll realize that my Father in heaven cares for
even this fight.

saturday

Coffee and tea let's meet up at three!
We'll sit outside the café under that big old tree,
And chat and laugh so stress free.

Through the leaves blows a summer breeze!
While through the air fly happy summer bees,
And with each windy gust a flower bows.

Through the shop windows the goods we'll
browse!
Within our hearts joy brews,
As in our minds each joyful moment burrows.

happy

With bright sticky notes and high hopes

In my mind I fight the foes

Of negative thoughts and dark lows

Simply writing down truths I know

So in my mind the seed of positivity can grow

And by my hand happiness flow

www.ingramcontent.com/pod-product-compliance
Lightning Source LLC
La Vergne TN
LVHW050309200726